Rewiring Reality

Rewiring Reality

The Power of Conscious Thought

Dr Livingston Rathanaraj

Dr Livingston

CONTENTS

CONTENTS

Introduction:

"Imagine a world where the power of your thoughts could reshape your reality. A world where conscious thinking becomes the catalyst for transformation, where the boundaries of what is possible are shattered, and where you hold the key to unlocking a life of limitless potential. Welcome to 'Rewiring Reality: The Power of Conscious Thought.'

In the words of renowned philosopher Henry David Thoreau, 'As a single footstep will not make a path on the earth, so a single thought will not make a pathway in mind. To make a deep physical path, we walk again and again. To make a deep mental path, we must think over and over the thoughts we wish to dominate our lives.'

In this book, we embark on a compelling journey into our thoughts' extraordinary influence over our reality. Together, we will explore the profound concept of conscious thought and how it can shape every aspect of our existence. By rewiring our minds, we hold the power to create a new reality, break free from limitations, and manifest our deepest desires.

The purpose of 'Rewiring Reality' is to provide you with a transformative roadmap to harness the power of conscious thought. As you turn these pages, you can expect to gain insights, practical tools, and empowering techniques that will enable you to take charge of your thoughts, reshape your reality, and live a life of abundance and fulfilment.

My own journey into the exploration of the power of thoughts was born out of deeply personal motivation. Growing up, I often found myself trapped in the confines of self-doubt, fear, and limiting beliefs. I witnessed the impact of negative thought patterns on my relationships, career, and overall sense of well-being. Frustrated by this self-imposed imprisonment, I embarked on a quest to understand the true potential of my mind.

Through years of research, introspection, and the guidance of brilliant mentors, I discovered the transformative power of conscious thought. I witnessed first-hand the extraordinary shifts that occurred when I consciously chose to empower my thoughts and redirect my focus towards positive outcomes. As I rewired my reality through conscious thought, my life blossomed in ways I had never imagined possible.

In 'Rewiring Reality,' I share not only the knowledge and wisdom gathered through my own journey but also the stories of individuals from all walks of life who have experienced profound transformations through the power of their thoughts. Their stories serve as a testament to the untapped potential within each of us and provide inspiration for the path ahead.

As we delve into the pages of this book, we will explore the mechanics of conscious thought, delve into the subconscious mind, and learn practical techniques to reprogram our thought patterns.

We will uncover the keys to manifesting our desires, creating harmonious relationships, and cultivating a deep sense of purpose and fulfilment.

So, I invite you to embark on this transformative journey with me. Together, let us harness the power of conscious thought to rewrite our stories, reshape our reality, and unlock a life of infinite possibilities. Get ready to discover the extraordinary potential that lies within you as we embark on the path of 'Rewiring Reality: The Power of Conscious Thought.'"

2

The Power of Conscious Thought: Understanding Thoughts and Their Influence

Defining Thoughts and Their Perceptual Impact

Thoughts have an extraordinary ability to shape our perception of the world around us. But what exactly are thoughts, and how do they influence our experiences? In this chapter, we will delve into the profound realm of conscious thought and explore its remarkable influence on our lives.

Thoughts can be understood as the mental processes of generating ideas, beliefs, and interpretations within our minds. They arise from the intricate workings of our brains, weaving a tapestry of perceptions that colour our reality. Each thought carries the power to shape our understanding, influence our emotions, and drive our behaviours.

Our perception of the world is not merely a reflection of objective reality but is filtered through the lens of our thoughts.

Imagine standing on a mountaintop, gazing at a breath taking sunset. While the beauty of the scene may appear universally stunning, the thoughts we attach to the experience can vary greatly.

One person may be filled with a sense of awe and gratitude, while another might feel a tinge of melancholy triggered by memories associated with sunsets.

The same external event elicits diverse internal responses based on our thoughts.

The Interplay Between Thoughts, Emotions, and Behaviours

Thoughts, emotions, and behaviours are intricately intertwined, creating a dynamic interplay within our lives. Our thoughts generate emotions, and these emotions, in turn, shape our behaviours. Consider a simple example: if we entertain positive thoughts about our abilities, we are more likely to experience feelings of confidence and competence, which can propel us to take bold actions. Conversely, if we harbour negative thoughts, self-doubt and fear may hinder our potential and limit our actions.

This interconnection between thoughts, emotions, and behaviours forms the foundation of the power of conscious thought. By becoming aware of our thoughts and intentionally directing them towards positive and empowering narratives, we can reshape our emotional experiences and align our behaviours with our desired outcomes. The power lies within our ability to choose our thoughts consciously and deliberately, steering our lives in the direction we envision.

The Role of Subconscious Thoughts and Their Impact

While conscious thoughts play a significant role in our lives, we must also recognize the influence of subconscious thoughts. Our subconscious mind operates beneath the surface of our awareness, quietly shaping our thoughts, beliefs, and behaviours. Often, these subconscious patterns stem from past experiences, societal conditioning, and deeply ingrained beliefs.

Exploring and understanding our subconscious thoughts is a crucial aspect of rewiring our reality. By bringing these hidden thoughts into conscious awareness, we can examine their validity and determine whether they align with our current desires and aspirations. Through mindfulness and introspection, we can identify and challenge limiting subconscious patterns, replacing them with thoughts that support our growth and well-being.

Scientific Research and Theories Supporting the Influence of Thoughts

The influence of thoughts on our experiences is not merely a philosophical concept; it is supported by a wealth of scientific research and theories. Scientists, psychologists, and researchers from various disciplines have delved into the fascinating realm of consciousness, cognition, and the power of thought.

Numerous studies have demonstrated the impact of thoughts on various aspects of our lives, including physical health, emotional well-being, and performance. Research on the placebo effect, for instance, reveals how the power of belief and positive thoughts can lead to tangible improvements in health outcomes. Additionally, cognitive-behavioural therapies have showcased the effectiveness of consciously changing thoughts to alleviate mental health disorders and enhance overall well-being.

Throughout this book, we will explore these scientific findings and theories, delving into the neuroscience, psychology, and quantum physics that support the profound influence of thoughts. Understanding the scientific basis behind the power of conscious thought strengthens our conviction and empowers us to embrace this transformative journey fully.

As we conclude this chapter, we now grasp the significance of thoughts in shaping our perceptions, emotions, and behaviours. We recognize the role of both conscious and subconscious thoughts, and we understand that scientific research supports the transformative potential of conscious thought.

In the following chapters, we will dive deeper into the practical aspects of rewiring our reality through conscious thought. We will explore techniques, exercises, and mindfulness practices that enable us to harness the power of our thoughts and align them with our deepest desires. Get ready to embark on a remarkable journey of self-discovery, empowerment, and transformation as we unveil the limitless possibilities that lie within the power of conscious thought.

Explaining Chapter 1 with a small story would be good. Let us understand through a story. Once upon a time, in a bustling city filled with people going about their daily lives, there lived a young woman named Maya. Maya was like any other person, navigating through the joys and challenges of life. However, she couldn't help but notice that some individuals seemed to have a different perspective, an inner radiance that set them apart.

One day, as Maya sat in a crowded coffee shop, she overheard a conversation between two strangers at a nearby table. One of them said, "You know, our thoughts have an incredible power over our lives. They shape our experiences and determine how we perceive the world around us." These words struck a chord within Maya, piquing her curiosity and igniting a desire to understand this power of thought.

Driven by this newfound intrigue, Maya embarked on a quest to unravel the mysteries of conscious thought. She sought to understand how thoughts shape our perceptions, emotions, and behaviours. As she delved into books, attended workshops, and engaged in conversations with experts, a fascinating world began to unfold before her.

Maya learned that thoughts are more than fleeting notions in our minds. They are the building blocks of our reality, the seeds from which our experiences grow. Thoughts have the incredible ability to colour our perception of the world. Just like a pair of tinted glasses, they can create a lens through which we see and interpret everything that happens around us.

She discovered the profound interplay between thoughts, emotions, and behaviours. When Maya thought positively and believed in her abilities, she noticed a surge of confidence and enthusiasm that fuelled her actions. On the other hand, when negative thoughts crept in, doubt and fear took hold, limiting her potential and stifling her dreams.

Curiosity led Maya further, urging her to explore the realm of subconscious thoughts. She realized that beneath the surface of her conscious mind, hidden patterns and beliefs quietly influenced her thoughts and actions. These subconscious patterns were like invisible threads woven into the fabric of her being, guiding her choices and shaping her reality.

Recognizing the importance of rewiring her reality, Maya delved into mindfulness and introspection. She began to pay attention to her thoughts, observing their origin and challenging those that no longer served her. With each conscious shift, she noticed how her emotions transformed and how her behaviours aligned with her true desires.

Maya's journey into the power of conscious thought was not a solitary one. Along her path, she encountered scientific research and theories that shed light on this phenomenon. Studies on the placebo effect demonstrated how thoughts and beliefs influenced physical healing. Cognitive-behavioural therapies showcased the effectiveness of consciously changing thoughts to improve mental health and overall well-being.

As Maya delved deeper into the science and practical aspects of conscious thought, she couldn't contain her excitement. She realized that understanding the influence of thoughts was not just a philosophical concept; it was a tangible reality supported by research and evidence. This knowledge fuelled her determination to harness the power of conscious thought and create a life of abundance and fulfilment.

As Chapter 1 drew to a close, Maya marvelled at the transformative potential lying within the realm of thoughts. She knew that her journey had only just begun. With a sense of gratitude and anticipation, she eagerly turned the page, ready to explore the practical techniques and exercises that would help her rewire her reality and unleash the limitless possibilities that lay within the power of conscious thought.

3

The Power of Conscious Thought: The Power of Positive Thinking

Understanding the Concept of Positive Thinking and Its Benefits

Positive thinking is like a beacon of light that illuminates our path towards a brighter and more fulfilling life. It is the conscious choice to focus on empowering thoughts, optimistic beliefs, and a hopeful outlook. In this chapter, we will delve into the profound impact of positive thinking and discover the transformative benefits it brings.

When we engage in positive thinking, we invite a wave of optimism into our lives. It allows us to see the potential for growth, resilience, and joy in every situation. Positive thinking nurtures a mindset of abundance, where we believe that possibilities are endless and that we have the power to shape our reality.

By adopting positive thinking, we unlock a treasure trove of benefits. Studies have shown that positive thinking enhances mental and emotional well-being. It reduces stress levels, boosts our immune system, and promotes a greater sense of happiness and contentment. Moreover, positive thinkers tend to have stronger relationships, increased resilience in the face of challenges, and a greater ability to attract success and abundance.

The Impact of Positive Thoughts on Mental and Emotional Well-being

Our thoughts have a profound influence on our mental and emotional well-being. When we cultivate positive thoughts, we create a nurturing environment for our minds and hearts to flourish. Positive thoughts fuel our self-esteem, cultivate self-compassion, and foster a sense of inner peace.

Negative thoughts, on the other hand, can weigh us down, leading to anxiety, self-doubt, and a pessimistic outlook on life. By consciously shifting our thoughts towards the positive, we can break free from the grip of negativity and create a foundation of mental and emotional resilience.

Through the power of positive thinking, we can reframe challenges as opportunities for growth, setbacks as lessons, and failures as stepping stones to success. It empowers us to rise above adversity and approach life with a sense of optimism and gratitude.

Practical Techniques to Cultivate Positive Thinking

Cultivating positive thinking is a skill that can be developed through consistent practice and intention. In this section, we will explore practical techniques that can help rewire our minds towards positivity and create a lasting shift in our thought patterns.

One effective technique is the practice of gratitude. By consciously acknowledging and appreciating the blessings in our lives, we shift our focus from lack to abundance, from negativity to positivity. Regularly journaling about what we are grateful for, expressing gratitude to others, or simply taking a few moments each day to reflect on our blessings can have a profound impact on our overall well-being.

Affirmations are another powerful tool for cultivating positive thinking. By repeating positive statements that reflect our desired beliefs and outcomes, we reprogram our subconscious mind and align it with our conscious intentions. Affirmations help us overcome self-limiting beliefs and instil a sense of confidence and empowerment.

Mindfulness and self-awareness are crucial in cultivating positive thinking. By becoming mindful of our thoughts, we can catch negative patterns as they arise and consciously redirect our focus towards more positive and empowering narratives. Meditation and mindfulness practices provide a space for self-reflection, allowing us to observe our thoughts without judgment and make intentional choices about the thoughts we cultivate.

Inspiring Stories of Transformation Through Positive Thinking

Throughout history, countless individuals have harnessed the power of positive thinking to transform their lives. In this section, we will explore inspiring stories of individuals who overcame adversity, embraced positive thinking, and created remarkable changes in their personal and professional lives.

From entrepreneurs who turned their failures into successes to athletes who visualized their victories, these stories serve as beacons of hope and inspiration. They remind us that we have the capacity to rewrite our narratives, break free from self-imposed limitations, and create a reality that aligns with our dreams and aspirations.

As we conclude Chapter 2, the power of positive thinking becomes evident. It has the potential to uplift our mental and emotional well-being, shape our experiences, and transform our lives. Armed with practical techniques and inspired by the stories of those who have walked this path, we are ready to embrace the power of positive thinking and embark on a journey of personal transformation and growth.

Once upon a time, in a small village nestled amidst rolling hills, there lived a young woman named Maya. Maya was known for her vibrant spirit and unwavering optimism. She seemed to radiate positivity, and her infectious smile brightened the lives of those around her.

Maya's positive outlook on life wasn't just a mere disposition; it was a conscious choice she made every day. She understood the profound impact that positive thinking had on her well-being and overall happiness. And so, she embarked on a journey to explore the true power of positive thinking.

Maya discovered that positive thinking was more than just wishful thinking or blind optimism. It was about consciously directing her thoughts towards empowering and uplifting narratives. Positive thinking allowed her to see the silver linings in every situation, no matter how challenging or difficult it might be.

The impact of positive thoughts on Maya's mental and emotional well-being was remarkable. She found that when she focused on the positive aspects of her life, her stress levels decreased, and a sense of calm washed over her. It was as if the weight of the world had lifted from her shoulders, and she could see clearly with renewed clarity and perspective.

Maya knew that positive thinking wasn't about denying or suppressing negative emotions; it was about acknowledging them and choosing to respond in a more constructive way. By consciously reframing her challenges as opportunities for growth and learning, she transformed setbacks into stepping stones toward success.

To cultivate positive thinking, Maya practised various techniques that she discovered along her journey. One technique was the practice of gratitude. Every evening, she would sit quietly and reflect on the things she was grateful for, both big and small. This simple act of acknowledging her blessings shifted her focus from what was lacking to what was abundant in her life.

Another technique Maya embraced was the use of affirmations. She would repeat positive statements to herself, such as "I am capable and deserving of success" or "Every day, I grow stronger and wiser." These affirmations helped her reprogram her subconscious mind, replacing self-doubt with self-belief and fostering a sense of empowerment.

Mindfulness played a significant role in Maya's practice of positive thinking. She learned to be present in each moment, fully aware of her thoughts and emotions. When negative thoughts arose, she didn't judge herself but instead gently redirected her focus towards more positive and empowering narratives. Through meditation and mindfulness exercises, Maya developed a deep sense of self-awareness and an ability to consciously choose the thoughts that shaped her reality.

Inspired by the stories she encountered along her journey, Maya discovered that countless individuals had transformed their lives through the power of positive thinking. She read about entrepreneurs who turned failures into successes, athletes who visualized their victories, and individuals who overcame seemingly insurmountable odds with unwavering optimism. These stories served as beacons of hope, reminding her that she, too, had the power to rewrite her story and create a reality that aligned with her dreams and aspirations.

As Chapter 2 drew to a close, Maya felt a renewed sense of purpose and determination. She realized that positive thinking was not just a fleeting notion; it was a transformative way of life. With gratitude in her heart and affirmations on her lips, she stepped into a world brimming with possibilities. Maya was ready to embrace the power of positive thinking, confident that it would guide her towards a life filled with joy, abundance, and fulfilment.

4

The Power of Conscious Thought: Overcoming Negative Thinking

The Dark Cloud of Negative Thinking

In a world where thoughts hold immense power, there existed a hidden realm known as the Kingdom of Negativity. This kingdom thrived on the destructive forces of negative thinking, wreaking havoc on the mental health and personal growth of its inhabitants.

As we venture into this chapter, we will explore the detrimental effects of negative thinking on the kingdom's residents. We will witness how their mental health suffered, leaving them trapped in a cycle of despair and self-doubt. Their dreams and aspirations were stifled, and their relationships strained under the weight of negativity.

Unraveling the Patterns

In our quest to understand the origins of negative thinking, we will journey deep into the labyrinth of the subconscious mind.

Here, we will uncover the common patterns that fuel the kingdom's negativity, tracing them back to their roots.

Through introspection and research, we will discover how past experiences, societal influences, and self-imposed expectations contribute to the development of negative thinking patterns. We will witness how the belief that one is unworthy or the fear of failure takes hold and shapes the thoughts that govern the lives of its inhabitants.

Shifting the Paradigm

But fear not, for the inhabitants of the Kingdom of Negativity are not without hope. In this section, we will learn powerful strategies and exercises that can challenge and reframe negative thoughts, paving the way for a brighter future.

We will delve into the art of cognitive restructuring, where we dismantle the walls built by negative thinking and replace them with new, empowering beliefs. Through this process, we will witness the transformation of self-doubt into self-confidence and fear into courage.

Additionally, we will explore the role of mindfulness in overcoming negative thinking. By cultivating a state of present-moment awareness, we can observe our thoughts without judgment and create space for new possibilities. Through mindfulness exercises and meditation, we will learn to redirect our focus from negativity to gratitude and compassion.

Stories of Triumph

As we near the end of this chapter, we will be inspired by personal anecdotes and case studies of individuals who have triumphed over the stronghold of negative thinking. Their stories will serve as beacons of light, guiding us through the darkest corners of our own minds.

We will meet Sarah, who battled crippling self-doubt but found the strength to challenge her negative beliefs. Through therapy, self-reflection, and unwavering determination, she rewired her thinking patterns, ultimately embracing her worth and finding fulfilment.

We will also encounter Mark, who faced countless setbacks and failures. Despite the weight of negativity, Mark refused to succumb. He embarked on a journey of self-discovery, reframing his experiences as valuable lessons and stepping stones toward success. Through his resilience and unwavering belief in himself, he shattered the chains of negative thinking and embraced a life filled with growth and achievement.

In sharing these stories, we aim to ignite a spark of hope within our readers. May their triumphs serve as a reminder that it is possible to overcome negative thinking and create a reality brimming with positivity and limitless possibilities.

As we conclude Chapter 3, let us reflect on the transformative power of conscious thought. By addressing the detrimental effects of negative thinking, exploring its origins, and equipping ourselves with strategies to challenge and reframe negative thoughts, we can break free from the clutches of the Kingdom of Negativity. Let us take these lessons to heart as we continue our journey towards rewiring our reality, one thought at a time.

Once upon a time, in a land known as the Kingdom of Thoughts, there was a dark corner called the Realm of Negativity. It was a place where negative thinking reigned supreme, casting its gloomy shadow over the inhabitants' mental health and personal growth.

As we delve into this chapter, let us journey into the heart of this realm and witness the detrimental effects of negative thinking on the lives of its residents. We will meet characters who found themselves trapped in a cycle of despair and self-doubt, their dreams and aspirations suffocated by the weight of negativity. Their minds became battlegrounds of self-criticism, anxiety, and a constant sense of unworthiness.

But amidst the darkness, a glimmer of hope emerges. Our protagonist embarks on a quest to understand the origins of negative thinking and uncover strategies to break free from its grip. Together, let us follow in their footsteps and discover the transformative power of conscious thought.

As our journey progresses, we unravel the intricate patterns that feed the realm of negativity. We learn that the inhabitants' negative thoughts often stem from past experiences, societal influences, and self-imposed expectations. Beliefs such as "I'm not good enough", or the fear of failure take root in their minds, shaping their perception of themselves and the world around them.

Armed with this newfound knowledge, we explore the strategies and exercises that can challenge and reframe negative thoughts. Our protagonist discovers the art of cognitive restructuring, a process that involves dismantling the negative walls of self-doubt and replacing them with empowering beliefs. We witness the transformation of self-criticism into self-compassion and fear into courage.

But our journey does not end there. We delve into the realm of mindfulness, where our protagonist learns the power of present-moment awareness. By observing their thoughts without judgment, they create space for new perspectives and possibilities. Through mindfulness exercises and meditation, they redirect their focus from negativity to gratitude and kindness, slowly rewiring their thought patterns.

As our protagonist grows in their understanding and mastery of overcoming negative thinking, we encounter inspiring stories of individuals who have triumphed over their own inner battles. We meet Sarah, who once drowned in self-doubt but discovered the strength to challenge her negative beliefs. Through therapy and self-reflection, she rewired her thinking, ultimately embracing her worth and finding joy in life.

We also crossed paths with Mark, who faced numerous setbacks and failures. Despite the heavy burden of negativity, Mark refused to surrender. He embarked on a journey of self-discovery, reframing his experiences as valuable lessons and opportunities for growth. Through resilience and unwavering belief in himself, he shattered the chains of negative thinking and achieved remarkable success.

These stories serve as beacons of hope, reminding us that we, too, can overcome the realm of negativity. They inspire us to embrace the power of conscious thought, knowing that by addressing the detrimental effects of negative thinking, exploring its origins, and practising strategies to challenge and reframe our thoughts, we can rewrite our own stories.

As we conclude Chapter 3, let us carry the wisdom gained on our journey. May the triumphs of our protagonist and the characters we've encountered motivate us to forge a path toward a reality filled with positivity and limitless potential. Remember, we hold the power to overcome negative thinking and reshape our lives—one thought at a time.

5

The Power of Conscious Thought: Visualization and Manifestation

In a world where thoughts shape reality, there exists a powerful tool called visualization. It is a gateway to the realm of possibilities, where dreams and desires take shape before they manifest in the physical world. In this chapter, we will explore the profound influence of visualization on our thoughts and outcomes, unlocking the potential to manifest our deepest desires.

As we embark on this journey of visualization and manifestation, let us first understand the essence of this transformative practice. Visualization involves creating vivid mental images of the desired outcomes we wish to manifest in our lives. By engaging our senses and emotions in this process, we align our thoughts with the energy of what we want to attract.

Setting intentions plays a pivotal role in the manifestation process. When we set clear and focused intentions, we create a roadmap for our thoughts to follow. By directing our conscious and subconscious minds toward a specific outcome, we harness the power of our thoughts to shape our reality.

To make visualization and manifestation practices effective, it is crucial to employ techniques that amplify their impact. Throughout this chapter, we will explore various techniques, such as guided imagery, affirmations, and vision boards. These techniques serve as catalysts, enhancing our ability to connect with our desires and create a strong vibrational alignment.

Drawing inspiration from success stories, we will meet individuals who have harnessed the power of visualization to achieve their goals. Maya, a passionate artist, envisioned herself showcasing her artwork in prestigious galleries worldwide. Through focused visualization and unwavering belief, she manifested opportunities that propelled her career to unimaginable heights.

Similarly, we will encounter Mike, a dedicated athlete who dreamed of becoming an Olympic champion. By visualizing himself crossing the finish line, feeling the weight of the gold medal around his neck, and hearing the roar of the crowd, he ignited a fire within himself. His consistent visualization practice not only enhanced his performance but also attracted the right opportunities and support, leading him to stand atop the Olympic podium.

These success stories illustrate the transformative potential of visualization and manifestation. They inspire us to embrace this practice as a powerful tool to manifest our own desires, be it in the realms of career, relationships, health, or personal growth.

As we conclude this chapter, let us reflect on the profound influence of visualization and manifestation. By harnessing the power of conscious thought and setting clear intentions, we can create a blueprint for our dreams to manifest in our lives. Through effective visualization techniques and unwavering belief, we align our energy with the desires of our hearts, inviting synchronicities and opportunities that guide us towards the fulfilment of our goals.

Once upon a time, in a land where thoughts held immense power, there existed a hidden practice known as Visualization and Manifestation. It was a sacred art passed down through generations, known only to those who sought to harness the true potential of their thoughts and create their desired reality.

In this chapter, we embark on a magical journey into the realm of Visualization and Manifestation. Our protagonist, Maya, yearned to understand the secrets of this transformative practice and unlock her ability to manifest her deepest desires.

As Maya delved into the world of visualization, she discovered its profound influence on thoughts and outcomes. Visualization, she learned, was more than just daydreaming—it was a powerful tool that allowed her to create vivid mental images of her desired future. Through these images, she could connect with the essence of her dreams and align her thoughts with the energy needed to manifest them into reality.

Setting intentions became a pivotal part of Maya's journey. She realized that by clearly defining her desires and setting focused intentions, she could steer the course of her thoughts towards her desired outcomes. It was as if she had planted seeds in the fertile soil of her mind, nurturing them with unwavering belief and purpose.

To make her visualization and manifestation practices even more potent, Maya explored various techniques that heightened their impact. Guided imagery allowed her to immerse herself in a detailed mental landscape, where she could vividly experience her desired reality. Affirmations became her daily mantra, reinforcing positive beliefs and affirming her deservingness of the manifestations she sought. Creating a vision board became a sacred ritual, where she curated images and words that represented her dreams, serving as a visual reminder of what she aimed to attract.

In her quest for knowledge, Maya discovered the inspiring stories of individuals who had harnessed the power of visualization to achieve extraordinary feats. She met Lucas, an aspiring entrepreneur who visualized himself standing on stage, delivering a powerful TED talk that inspired thousands. Through his unwavering visualization practice, he not only attracted opportunities to share his message but also gained the confidence and clarity needed to create a successful business around his passion.

Similarly, Maya encountered Sarah, a young woman who envisioned herself living a life of vibrant health and vitality. Through her consistent visualization practice, Sarah transformed her mindset, aligning her thoughts with optimal well-being. Her visualizations guided her to make healthier choices, attract supportive relationships, and embark on a journey of self-care that led to a life filled with vitality and joy.

As Maya embraced the art of visualization and manifestation, she realized that she held the power to create her own reality. She understood that her thoughts were the seeds, and her intentions were the guiding force that shaped her experiences. With each visualization practice, she strengthened her connection to her dreams, feeling them draw closer with every passing day.

As we conclude this chapter, let us remember the transformative potential of visualization and manifestation. Through focused thoughts, clear intentions, and immersive techniques, we can unlock the magic within ourselves and manifest our deepest desires. Just like Maya, may we embrace this enchanting practice and tap into the power of our conscious thoughts, for within them lies the key to rewiring our reality and creating a life beyond our wildest dreams.

6 |

The Power of Conscious Thought: The Mind-Body Connection

In the vast landscape of our existence, where thoughts intertwine with the very essence of our being, lies a profound connection between the mind and the body. Welcome to the fifth chapter of our exploration, where we dive deep into the transformative power of conscious thought and its impact on our physical health. Prepare to witness the remarkable interplay between our thoughts and the well-being of our bodies.

As we embark on this enlightening journey, let us first unravel the link between thoughts and physical health. Our thoughts, like threads weaving through the tapestry of our lives, possess the power to shape our overall well-being. The quality of our thoughts directly influences the state of our bodies, moulding our experiences and affecting our physical health in profound ways.

One area where thoughts exert significant influence is stress. Negative thought patterns and the burdens of everyday life can tip the scales of our well-being, leading to elevated stress levels that impact our bodies at a cellular level. Conversely, cultivating positive thoughts and adopting a resilient mindset can enhance our ability to cope with stress, boost our immune function, and foster a state of overall well-being.

To shed light on this extraordinary connection, let us turn our gaze towards the remarkable findings of scientific research and studies. Through rigorous exploration, these studies have unearthed the intricate mechanisms through which our thoughts influence our physical health. They have revealed the profound impact of thoughts on our stress response, immune function, hormone balance, and even the rate of healing. The evidence is clear: our thoughts possess the power to shape our physical reality.

Equipped with this knowledge, we embark on a quest to harness the power of conscious thought to enhance our physical health. We begin by nurturing positive thoughts, cultivating a mindset of gratitude, and embracing practices that promote stress reduction. Mindfulness, meditation, and deep breathing exercises become our allies on this journey as we learn to centre ourselves, anchor our thoughts in the present moment, and create a harmonious balance between our minds and bodies.

Along our path, we encounter inspiring stories of individuals who have harnessed the mind-body connection to transform their lives. Meet Maya, who, through the power of positive affirmations and visualization, not only reduced her stress levels but also witnessed remarkable improvements in her immune function and overall well-being. Witnessing her journey serves as a testament to the incredible potential that lies within us to shape our physical health through conscious thought.

As we conclude this chapter, let us embrace the understanding that our thoughts hold the key to unlocking the full potential of our physical well-being. By nurturing positive thoughts, adopting stress-reducing practices, and cultivating a mindful approach to life, we can tap into the immense power of conscious thought to enhance our physical health and create a foundation for a vibrant life.

Once upon a time, in a world where thoughts held the power to shape destinies, there existed a remarkable connection between the mind and the body. In the enchanting fifth chapter of our odyssey, we embark on a captivating journey to unravel the secrets of the mind-body connection and discover the transformative influence of conscious thought on our physical health. Prepare to be enchanted by tales of wonder where thoughts weave their magic on the fabric of our well-being.

As we venture forth, let us uncover the invisible threads that bind our thoughts and physical health. Imagine a symphony where the harmonious interplay of thoughts orchestrates the melodies of our vitality. Our thoughts, like wisps of wind, carry the potential to sculpt our bodies and impact our well-being in profound ways.

One profound area where thoughts manifest their might is in the realm of stress. Negative thought patterns and the weight of life's burdens cast shadows upon our well-being, causing stress to ripple through our bodies like tumultuous waves. However, by embracing positive thoughts and fostering a resilient mindset, we can forge a shield against the storms of stress. In doing so, we unlock the power to strengthen our immune function, restore balance to our bodies, and cultivate a state of overall well-being.

To illuminate this captivating connection, let us unveil the scientific research and studies that serve as beacons of knowledge. These extraordinary endeavours have delved into the depths of the mind-body connection, unearthing a treasure trove of revelations. They have unravelled the intricate pathways through which our thoughts influence our physical health, showcasing the profound impact on stress levels, immune function, hormonal equilibrium, and even the pace of healing. Through their findings, we stand witness to the awe-inspiring truth that our thoughts hold power to shape our physical reality.

Equipped with this newfound wisdom, we embark on a quest to harness the enchanting power of conscious thought for our physical well-being. With each step, we learn to tend to the garden of our minds, nurturing positive thoughts and cultivating gratitude as fertile soil. We embrace practices that soothe our souls, such as mindfulness, meditation, and the rhythmic dance of deep breathing. These become the tools that empower us to find serenity, anchor our thoughts in the present moment, and forge a harmonious bond between our minds and bodies.

Amidst our journey, we encounter extraordinary tales of individuals who have unlocked the wonders of the mind-body connection. Let us meet Lucas, a radiant soul who, through the sheer power of positive affirmations and vivid visualization, not only diminished the weight of stress but also witnessed a wondrous transformation in his immune function and overall well-being. His story dances like a sunbeam, reminding us of the boundless potential that lies within each of us to shape our physical health through the alchemy of conscious thought.

As we bid adieu to this chapter, let us carry with us the understanding that our thoughts hold the key to unlocking the full radiance of our physical well-being. By embracing positive thoughts, weaving stress-reducing practices into the tapestry of our lives, and embracing the art of mindful living, we unleash the extraordinary power of conscious thought to enhance our physical health and nurture a vibrant existence.

In the next chapter of our extraordinary voyage, we embark upon the realm of personal transformation. Prepare to delve into the boundless horizons where our thoughts shape our identities, beliefs, and the very fabric of reality we perceive. Brace yourself for a tale of self-discovery and empowerment as we unveil the extraordinary capacity of our thoughts to rewire the very essence of our existence.

Cultivating a Mindful Mindset

In the bustling tapestry of life, where thoughts flutter like delicate butterflies, there exists a transformative practice that holds the key to unlocking the true power of conscious thought. Welcome to the sixth chapter of our voyage, where we embark on a serene exploration of cultivating a mindful mindset. Prepare to discover the art of mindful living and witness the profound impact it has on harnessing the limitless potential of our thoughts.

As we delve into the depths of this chapter, let us acknowledge the significance of mindfulness in harnessing the power of our thoughts. Picture a tranquil lake, it's surface undisturbed by the ripples of distraction. Mindfulness, like a serene reflection upon the water's edge, invites us to observe our thoughts with clarity and intention. By cultivating a mindful mindset, we become conscious observers of our thoughts, gaining mastery over their influence on our lives.

Let us now embark on a journey to explore the techniques that allow us to observe and regulate our thoughts with mindfulness.

Like a gentle breeze guiding a sail, mindfulness offers us the tools to navigate the vast ocean of our consciousness. Through practices such as meditation, breath awareness, and body scans, we develop the capacity to witness our thoughts without judgment or attachment. We learn to acknowledge their presence and gently guide them towards a state of serenity and clarity.

As we immerse ourselves in the realm of mindfulness, we encounter a myriad of benefits that extend far beyond the boundaries of our thoughts. The practice of mindfulness serves as an anchor amidst the storms of life, reducing stress and fostering a sense of calm. By cultivating a mindful mindset, we unlock the power to nurture our focus and enhance our ability to engage fully in the present moment. Through mindfulness, we cultivate resilience, emotional well-being, and a deep sense of inner peace.

To truly integrate the power of mindfulness into our daily lives, let us embark on a path of guidance and practicality. We learn to infuse mindful awareness into every aspect of our existence, from the simplest of tasks to the most profound experiences. We engage in mindful eating, savouring each bite and cultivating a deeper connection with our nourishment. We embrace mindful movement, allowing our bodies to express themselves freely in the present moment. Through the gentle art of mindfulness, we weave a tapestry of conscious living, transforming every moment into an opportunity for growth and self-discovery.

As we conclude this chapter, let us carry the essence of mindfulness within our hearts and minds. By cultivating a mindful mindset, we become architects of our thoughts, shaping our reality with intention and grace. The power of conscious thought intertwines with the practice of mindfulness, birthing a harmonious symphony that reverberates through every aspect of our being.

In the upcoming chapter of our extraordinary voyage, we embark upon a quest to explore the uncharted territories of resilience and personal growth. Brace yourself for an adventure filled with tales of courage, resilience, and the unwavering spirit of human potential. Together, we will unveil the transformative power that lies within us to overcome challenges, reframe our narratives, and manifest our wildest dreams. Get ready to witness the awe-inspiring journey of rewiring reality through the prism of resilience.

Once upon a time, in a world where thoughts held the power to shape destinies, there existed a realm of mindfulness that illuminated the path to harnessing the extraordinary potential of conscious thought. In the enchanting sixth chapter of our odyssey, we embark on a captivating journey into the realm of cultivating a mindful mindset. Prepare to be transported to a place where time slows down and the wisdom of the present moment unfolds before your very eyes.

In the bustling village of life, amidst the clamour of thoughts and distractions, there lived a wise sage named Maya. Maya understood the transformative power of mindfulness and its profound impact on the tapestry of thoughts that coloured the lives of the villagers. She knew that by cultivating a mindful mindset, they could unlock the boundless potential of their conscious thoughts and transform their realities.

One beautiful morning, Maya gathered the villagers beneath the shade of a towering oak tree. The air was filled with anticipation as they gathered around, eager to learn the art of mindful living. With a warm smile, Maya began to share the importance of mindfulness in harnessing the power of thoughts.

"Imagine," she said, "that your thoughts are like the leaves that dance in the wind. They have the power to sway your emotions, shape your actions, and paint the canvas of your life. But through mindfulness, we can become the gentle observers of our thoughts, allowing us to navigate the vast landscape of our minds with clarity and intention."

As the villagers listened attentively, Maya guided them through the techniques of mindfulness. She encouraged them to sit in stillness, to close their eyes, and to bring their awareness to their breath. With each inhales and exhale, they connected with the present moment, letting go of worries and distractions. They observed their thoughts, acknowledging their presence without judgment and gently guiding their minds back to the tranquillity of their breath.

With each passing day, the villagers embraced the practice of mindfulness in their lives. They discovered the profound impact it had on their well-being, as stress melted away like dewdrops in the morning sun. They marvelled at how their focus sharpened, allowing them to engage fully in each task and experience the richness of the present moment.

Maya shared stories of individuals who had woven mindfulness into the fabric of their lives, transforming their realities with its gentle touch. There was Alex, who once carried the weight of stress and anxiety, but through the practice of mindfulness, found inner peace and emotional resilience. And then there was Maya, who embraced mindful eating, savouring each bite and cultivating a deeper connection with her nourishment, leading to improved digestion and overall well-being.

The villagers were inspired by these tales of transformation, and with newfound determination, they incorporated mindfulness into every aspect of their existence. They savoured the taste of their meals, feeling the textures and flavours dance upon their tongues. They took mindful walks in nature, feeling the earth beneath their feet and connecting with the beauty around them. In each moment, they found an opportunity for growth and self-discovery, their mindful mindset guiding them towards a life of profound fulfilment.

As the sun began to set on that day, the villagers gathered once more beneath the oak tree, gratitude shining in their eyes. They thanked Maya for sharing the wisdom of mindfulness and for guiding them on this transformative journey of rewiring their reality through the prism of a mindful mindset.

In the upcoming chapter of our extraordinary voyage, we venture into the uncharted territories of resilience and personal growth. Join us as we delve into the stories of individuals who have overcome adversity, reframed their narratives, and manifested their dreams through the unwavering power of conscious thought. Brace yourself for a tale of courage and resilience, where the human spirit soars above the challenges that come their way. Get ready to witness the remarkable journey of rewiring reality through the eyes of those who embody the essence of resilience.

8 |

Thoughts and Relationships

In the intricate tapestry of human connections, where hearts intertwine, and souls dance, lies a profound truth: our thoughts hold the power to shape the very essence of our relationships. Welcome to the seventh chapter of our transformative journey, where we unravel the intricate threads that bind thoughts and relationships together. Prepare to explore the profound impact our thoughts have on the tapestry of our connections and discover the key to cultivating fulfilling and harmonious relationships.

As we embark on this chapter, let us dive into the depths of how thoughts influence our interactions and relationships with others. Imagine a gentle breeze whispering through a field of flowers, its touch influencing the petals' sway. Similarly, our thoughts create the energetic currents that shape the way we perceive and engage with those around us. By understanding the power of our thoughts in relationships, we unlock the potential to build bridges of understanding and empathy.

Communication, the lifeblood of relationships, plays a pivotal role in maintaining their health and vitality. Our self-perception, influenced by our thoughts, shapes the way we communicate and connect with others. Like a mirror reflecting our inner landscape, our thoughts colour the lens through which we perceive ourselves and others. By cultivating positive thoughts, we create a fertile ground for open and authentic communication, fostering trust, compassion, and mutual respect.

Within the realm of relationships, our thoughts shape the narrative we construct, the stories we tell ourselves and others. Like skilled storytellers, we have the power to reshape these narratives by changing our thoughts. Through conscious awareness, we can challenge limiting beliefs, dissolve judgments, and embrace a more compassionate and understanding perspective. By rewiring our thoughts, we invite transformation, healing, and the possibility of deeper and more meaningful connections.

Let us now explore practical strategies for improving communication by cultivating positive thoughts. Like nurturing a garden, we tend to the seeds of kindness, empathy, and gratitude within our minds. We practice active listening, offering our undivided attention to those we engage with. We choose our words wisely, expressing ourselves with clarity and sensitivity. We let go of assumptions and allow curiosity to guide our interactions, fostering a space for authentic and heartfelt communication to flourish.

As we venture further into this chapter, let us draw inspiration from real-life examples that illustrate the transformative power of changing our thoughts. Meet Emily and James, a couple whose relationship was once plagued by misunderstandings and conflict.

Through introspection and a shift in their thought patterns, they discovered a newfound understanding, deepening their love and connection. Witnessing their transformation, we glimpse the extraordinary potential that lies within each of us to reshape our relationships through the power of conscious thought.

In Conclusion, let us embrace the realization that our thoughts are the sculptors of our relationships. With intention and mindfulness, we can cultivate positive thoughts, reframe narratives, and communicate with authenticity and compassion. By rewiring our thought patterns, we breathe new life into our connections, fostering harmony and creating a space where love and understanding can flourish.

As we embark on the final leg of our extraordinary voyage, we traverse the terrain of personal transformation and self-empowerment. Brace yourself for a chapter filled with tales of self-discovery, inner strength, and the unwavering spirit of human potential. Together, we will unravel the mysteries of self-empowerment and witness the incredible capacity we possess to shape our realities through conscious thought. Get ready to embark on a journey where the power to rewire reality lies within your hands.

Once upon a time, in a world where thoughts wove the intricate tapestry of relationships, there existed a village nestled amidst rolling hills. In this village, the power of conscious thought was about to unveil its secrets, particularly in the enchanting seventh chapter of our tale. Join us on a captivating journey as we explore the profound connection between thoughts and relationships, and discover the key to cultivating harmonious and fulfilling connections with others.

In the heart of the village, there lived a wise elder named Maya. Maya understood the delicate dance between thoughts and relationships, and she held the key to unlocking the transformative potential that lay within. Eager to share this wisdom with the villagers, Maya gathered them beneath a majestic oak tree, where stories of hope and transformation had been shared for generations.

With a warm smile, Maya began to weave a tale of how thoughts influence our interactions and relationships with others. She compared thoughts to the gentle breeze that rustles through a meadow, shaping the way we perceive and engage with the world around us. The villagers listened intently, their curiosity piqued, as Maya unveiled the immense power hidden within their thoughts.

As the sun cast its golden glow upon the gathering, Maya delved deeper into the role of communication and self-perception in maintaining healthy relationships. She spoke of the importance of self-awareness and how our thoughts shape the way we communicate and connect with others. Like a mirror reflecting our inner world, our thoughts colour the lens through which we view ourselves and those around us. Maya emphasized that by cultivating positive thoughts, we create an environment where open and authentic communication can thrive, fostering trust, understanding, and harmony.

With each word Maya spoke, the villagers felt a sense of hope and possibility stirring within their hearts. They yearned to transform their relationships, dissolve barriers and create deeper connections. Maya shared practical strategies for improving communication by cultivating positive thoughts. She encouraged the villagers to tend to the seeds of kindness, empathy, and gratitude within their minds, nurturing a fertile ground for heartfelt communication to blossom. The villagers were inspired to become active listeners, offering their undivided attention to those they engaged with. They vowed to choose their words wisely, expressing themselves with clarity and sensitivity. They embraced curiosity, letting go of assumptions and embracing a genuine desire to understand one another.

As the villagers absorbed the wisdom Maya shared, their hearts swelled with anticipation. They longed for real-life examples that would illuminate the transformative power of changing their thoughts. Maya began to share stories of individuals who had rewritten their relationship narratives through conscious thought. They listened with awe as Emily and James, a couple plagued by misunderstandings and conflict, discovered a profound understanding and deepened their love by shifting their thought patterns. These stories ignited a flame of hope within the villagers, showing them that they, too, possessed the power to reshape their relationships through conscious thought.

With gratitude in their hearts, the villagers bid farewell to Maya, feeling empowered and eager to embark on their own journeys of transformation. They knew that the path ahead might hold challenges, but armed with the knowledge of the mind's influence on relationships, they were determined to forge deeper connections rooted in understanding and love.

As the sun began to set, casting a warm glow over the village, the villagers made a pact to continue their exploration of the power of conscious thought. They understood that thoughts were not mere whispers in the wind but potent forces that could reshape their reality. With renewed purpose and a sense of unity, they looked ahead to the final chapter of their extraordinary voyage, where the journey of self-empowerment and personal transformation awaited them.

Join us as we set foot into the realm of self-discovery and inner strength, where the power to rewire reality lies within the grasp of every individual. Brace yourself for a chapter filled with tales of resilience, courage, and the boundless potential that resides within us all. Together, we will unlock the secrets of self-empowerment and witness the extraordinary capacity we possess to shape our realities through conscious thought. Get ready to embrace the magic that awaits as we continue our journey through the pages of Rewiring Reality.

9 |

Conclusion:

As we reach the final chapter of Rewiring Reality, it is time to reflect on the transformative journey we have embarked upon and distil its essence into a tapestry of wisdom. Throughout this book, we have explored the extraordinary power of conscious thought and its potential to shape every facet of our lives. Let us take a moment to recap the key points and takeaways that will forever resonate within our hearts and minds.

First and foremost, we have come to understand that thoughts are not mere fleeting fragments of our consciousness; they are the architects of our reality. They shape our perception of the world, influence our emotions and behaviours, and hold the key to unlocking our true potential. We have witnessed how negative thoughts can hinder our growth, while positive thoughts have the ability to uplift and transform our lives.

In the realm of relationships, we have discovered that our thoughts act as a powerful force, either building bridges of understanding or erecting barriers of misunderstanding. By cultivating positive thoughts and practising mindful communication, we can foster deeper connections, enriching our relationships with love, empathy, and authenticity.

The mind-body connection has been illuminated, revealing the profound impact our thoughts have on our physical well-being. Stress, immune function, and overall health are intricately intertwined with our thoughts. By harnessing the power of our thoughts, we can reduce stress, boost our immune system, and enhance our overall well-being.

Throughout our exploration, scientific research and studies have provided a solid foundation for understanding the influence of thoughts. We have delved into the realms of positive psychology, mindfulness, and visualization, uncovering evidence that supports the transformative potential of conscious thought. These findings serve as a reminder that our journey is not a mere flight of fancy but is grounded in scientific principles.

As we conclude this book, let us not simply close its pages and move on. Instead, let us carry the torch of knowledge and apply the concepts and techniques we have learned. The power of rewiring reality lies within each of us, waiting to be harnessed and unleashed. Take a moment to pause, breathe, and reflect on the possibilities that await you when you consciously choose your thoughts.

To aid you on your ongoing journey of self-discovery and personal transformation, we offer additional resources and recommended readings. These will serve as guideposts along the path, further deepening your understanding and expanding your horizons. Remember, the quest for rewiring reality is a lifelong endeavour, and these resources will be your companions on this extraordinary voyage.

As we bid farewell, let us carry the wisdom of rewiring reality in our hearts and minds. Embrace the power of conscious thought, for it is the key that unlocks the doors to a world of infinite possibilities. May you continue to cultivate positive thoughts, nourish your relationships, and enhance every aspect of your life through the transformative potential of rewiring reality.

Thank you for joining us on this extraordinary journey, and may your future be filled with joy, abundance, and the unyielding spirit of conscious thought.

Once upon a time, in a land where thoughts held the power to shape reality, there existed a village of seekers. These seekers had embarked on a profound journey through the pages of a book called Rewiring Reality, guided by the wisdom of Dr Livingston. As they reached the final chapter, the Conclusion, their hearts brimmed with anticipation, eager to distil the transformative lessons learned and embrace the magic that awaited them.

Gathered beneath the sheltering branches of an ancient tree, the seekers listened attentively as Dr Livingston wove their collective experiences into a tapestry of reflection. The village buzzed with excitement as they prepared to embark on the final leg of their voyage.

Dr Livingston began by reminding the seekers of the remarkable power their thoughts held. They were the architects of their reality, capable of moulding their perceptions, emotions, and behaviours.

Negative thoughts could cast a shadow, but positive thoughts hold the potential to uplift and transform lives.

Delving deeper into the realm of relationships, Dr Livingston unveiled the intricate connection between thoughts and human connections. The seekers understood that their thoughts, like an invisible thread, wove the tapestry of their interactions. By cultivating positive thoughts and embracing mindful communication, they could build bridges of understanding and compassion, fostering deeper connections filled with love, empathy, and authenticity.

As the seekers listened with rapt attention, Dr Livingston revealed the astonishing mind-body connection. Thoughts, it seemed, had the power to influence physical health. Stress, immune function, and overall well-being were intertwined with the thoughts they nurtured. The seekers were in awe of the revelations, realizing that by harnessing the power of their thoughts, they could reduce stress, boost their immune systems, and enhance their overall well-being.

Throughout their journey, the seekers witnessed the scientific research and studies that supported the transformative potential of conscious thought. Dr Livingston shared these findings, offering a solid foundation for their understanding and igniting a renewed sense of conviction within their souls. This was not just a flight of fancy; it was a path grounded in scientific principles, a path they were now prepared to tread.

As the Conclusion drew near, Dr Livingston urged the seekers not to merely close the book and move on. The power of rewiring reality lay dormant within each of them, waiting to be harnessed. They were encouraged to apply the concepts and techniques they had learned, to consciously choose their thoughts, and become the architects of their destinies.

With a gentle smile, Dr Livingston presented the seekers with additional resources and recommended readings. These would serve as guideposts along their ongoing journey of self-discovery and personal transformation, helping them delve deeper, expand their horizons, and embrace the endless possibilities that lay before them.

As the village bid farewell to Dr Livingston, a profound silence enveloped the air. The seekers, their hearts ablaze with newfound wisdom, understood that their voyage had only just begun. They carried the torch of knowledge within their souls, ready to illuminate their path, nurture their relationships, and enhance every aspect of their lives through the transformative potential of rewiring reality.

The village dispersed, each seeker carrying the essence of the Conclusion in their hearts. They knew that the quest for rewiring reality was a lifelong endeavour, an extraordinary voyage of self-discovery. They were determined to cultivate positive thoughts, nourish their relationships, and embrace the boundless potential that lay within them.

And so, as they ventured forth, the seekers embraced their destiny with joy, abundance, and the unyielding spirit of conscious thought. Their journey had come full circle, but their story was far from over. With each passing day, they would continue to rewrite their realities, harnessing the power within and paving the way for a future brimming with infinite possibilities.

Author

Dr Livingston is a renowned expert in the field of consciousness and personal development. With a background in Sales and People Management and a passion for exploring the power of thoughts, Dr Livingston has dedicated their life to understanding and unlocking the transformative potential of conscious thought.

Throughout their career, Dr Livingston has conducted extensive research, collaborated with leading experts, and guided countless individuals on their journey of self-discovery and personal transformation. Their work has been recognized for its innovative insights and practical applications in rewiring reality.

Dr Livingston's mission is to empower individuals to harness the power of their thoughts and create extraordinary lives. Through their writing, speaking engagements, and workshops, they have inspired and guided people from all walks of life to cultivate positive thinking, enhance relationships, improve physical health, and manifest their deepest desires.

With a warm and compassionate approach, Dr Livingston combines scientific knowledge, practical techniques, and personal anecdotes to connect with readers on a profound level. Their writing style is accessible and engaging, making complex concepts easily understandable and relatable.

As an advocate for lifelong learning, Dr Livingston encourages readers to continue their exploration beyond the pages of the book. They provide additional resources, recommended readings, and guidance for further study, ensuring that the transformative journey continues long after the book is finished.

Whether you are a seeker on the path of personal growth or someone looking to unlock their true potential, Dr Livingston's insights and expertise will serve as a guiding light, illuminating the power of conscious thought and rewiring reality.

Join Dr Livingston on this extraordinary journey of self-discovery as they share their wisdom, experiences, and the tools to transform your life through the power of thoughts. Together, let us rewrite our realities and embrace a future filled with limitless possibilities.